America *the* Beautiful ★ *to* Color

Road Trip Adventures to Color

ZOË INGRAM

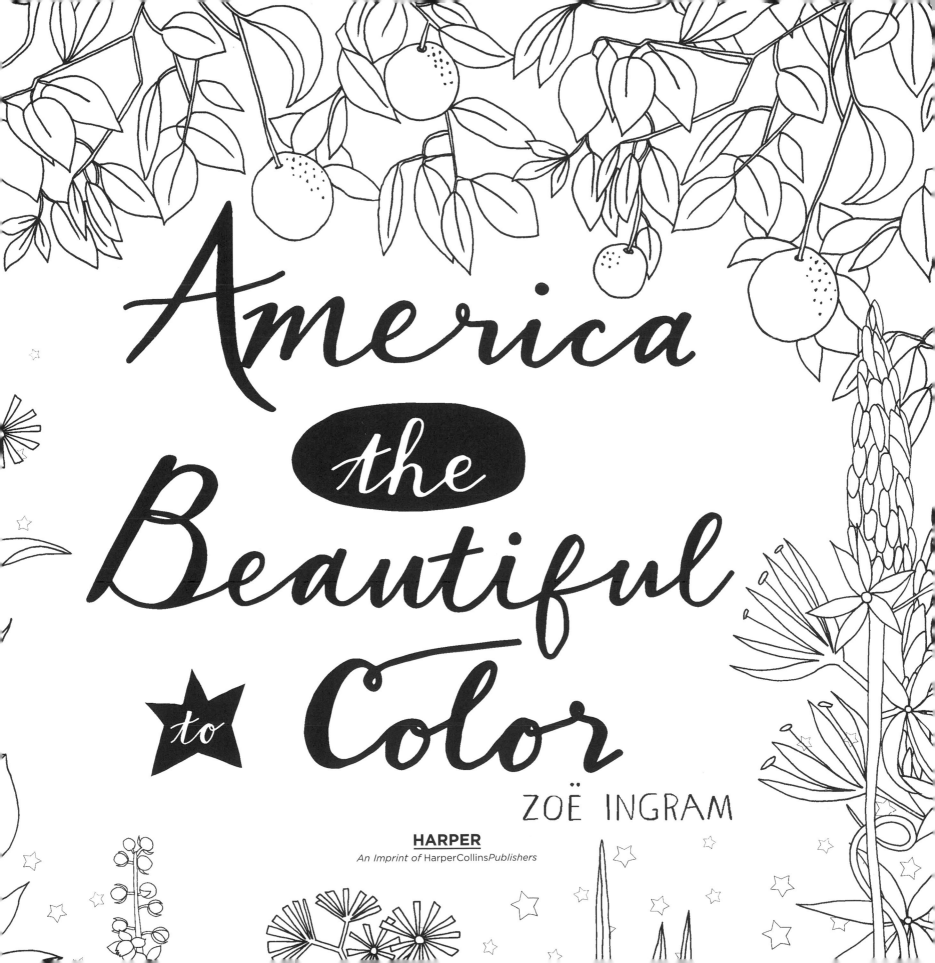

America the Beautiful to Color

ZOË INGRAM

HARPER
An Imprint of HarperCollins Publishers

Mark, let's go to Hawaii. —ZI

America the Beautiful to Color: Road Trip Adventures to Color

Copyright © 2017 by HarperCollins Publishers

All rights reserved. Printed in the United States of America.

No part of this book may be used or reproduced in any manner whatsoever without written permission except in the case of brief quotations embodied in critical articles and reviews. For information address HarperCollins Children's Books, a division of HarperCollins Publishers, 195 Broadway, New York, NY 10007.

www.harpercollinschildrens.com

ISBN 978-0-06-256990-5

The artist used pencil, fineliner pen, brush pen, and computer to create the illustrations for this book.

Typography by Celeste Knudsen

17 18 19 20 21 PC/LSCW 10 9 8 7 6 5 4 3 2 1

❖

First Edition

THIS BOOK BELONGS TO

_____

This book is an invitation to awaken your inner traveler. You'll find designs featuring the sights and scenes for an epic American road trip. Who knows, this book might lead you to your next adventure! See a rodeo, sleep in a tree house, or ride your bike down a country lane. From eagles soaring over Alaska to brass trumpets in New Orleans, from wildflowers on back roads to the Statue of Liberty, get ready to be transported to the amazing places that make up the America we cherish.

There are so many creative ways to enjoy this book. The choice is yours—experiment with colored pencils, gel pens, or felt-tip pens. Play with colors; there are no hard and fast rules and there's room to have fun. It's your book, so be as experimental as you please. Don't color as if there's someone looking over your shoulder. I hope you come away from coloring my book feeling inspired!

Zoë Ingram

My Influences

Doing my job is its own best inspiration—I love art and have wanted to be an artist since I was a small child. When I'm not working on art for a client, I'm usually painting and drawing for myself.

If I'm looking for visual inspiration, it's just outside! Bright colors and incredible flora and fauna are always great for a creative spark. I can just step outside my front door and see what inspiration strikes!

Behind the Scenes:
How I Create My Art to Color

I initially use a pencil for sketching out the rough outline of a piece.
After that, I like to vary my process! I might use brush pens for a
looser line or a wide variety of fineliner pens for a tighter line with
different thicknesses. I really like to experiment and try out new
techniques as I'm drawing. Finally, I scan my drawings in and use
some kind of digital program to clean up the art—to get rid of any
spare lines or smudges and make sure everything looks good.

A map to the perfect road trip—this genius route hits every state in the continental US without backtracking! Use this page to keep track of what you've colored—or where you've traveled!

Pacific Northwest and Alaska

- ☐ Alaska AK
- ☐ Washington WA
- ☐ Oregon OR
- ☐ Idaho ID

Western and Hawaii

- ☐ California CA
- ☐ Nevada NV
- ☐ Arizona AZ
- ☐ Hawaii HI

Rocky Mountain

- ☐ Montana MT
- ☐ North Dakota ND
- ☐ South Dakota SD
- ☐ Wyoming WY
- ☐ Colorado CO
- ☐ Utah UT

Southwest

- ☐ New Mexico NM
- ☐ Oklahoma OK
- ☐ Texas TX
- ☐ Arkansas AR
- ☐ Louisiana LA

Midwest

- ☐ Minnesota MN
- ☐ Wisconsin WI
- ☐ Iowa IA
- ☐ Michigan MI
- ☐ Kansas KS
- ☐ Nebraska NE

Missouri MO
- ☐ Missouri MO
- ☐ Illinois IL
- ☐ Indiana IN
- ☐ Ohio OH

North Atlantic

- ☐ Maine ME
- ☐ Rhode Island RI
- ☐ New Hampshire NH
- ☐ Vermont VT
- ☐ Massachusetts MA
- ☐ Connecticut CT
- ☐ New York NY

Mid-Atlantic

- ☐ Pennsylvania PA
- ☐ New Jersey NJ
- ☐ Delaware DE
- ☐ Maryland MD
- ☐ West Virginia WV
- ☐ Virginia VA
- ☐ Washington, DC

Southeast

- ☐ Kentucky KY
- ☐ Tennessee TN
- ☐ North Carolina NC
- ☐ South Carolina SC
- ☐ Georgia GA
- ☐ Alabama AL
- ☐ Mississippi MS
- ☐ Florida FL

O beautiful
for spacious skies
—KATHARINE LEE BATES

ALASKA

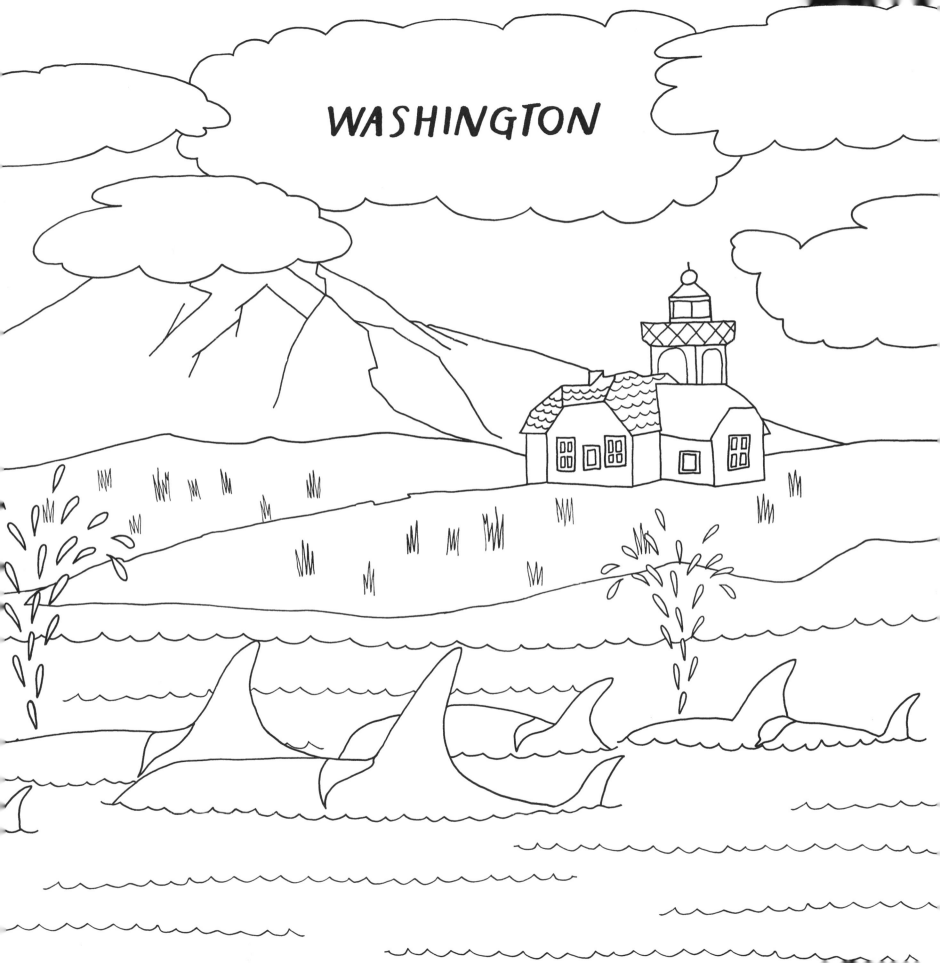

Get off
the
beaten path

IDAHO

CALIFORNIA dreaming!

FREE as the ROAD

—GEORGE HERBERT

ARIZONA

HAWAII

ROCKY MOUNTAIN

SOUTH DAKOTA

COLORADO

This Land Is Your Land

—WOODY GUTHRIE

UTAH

STEP ON THE

UTAH | COLORADO
ARIZONA | NEW MEXICO

FOUR CORNERS

NEW MEXICO

Ride
in a hot-air
balloon

LOUISIANA

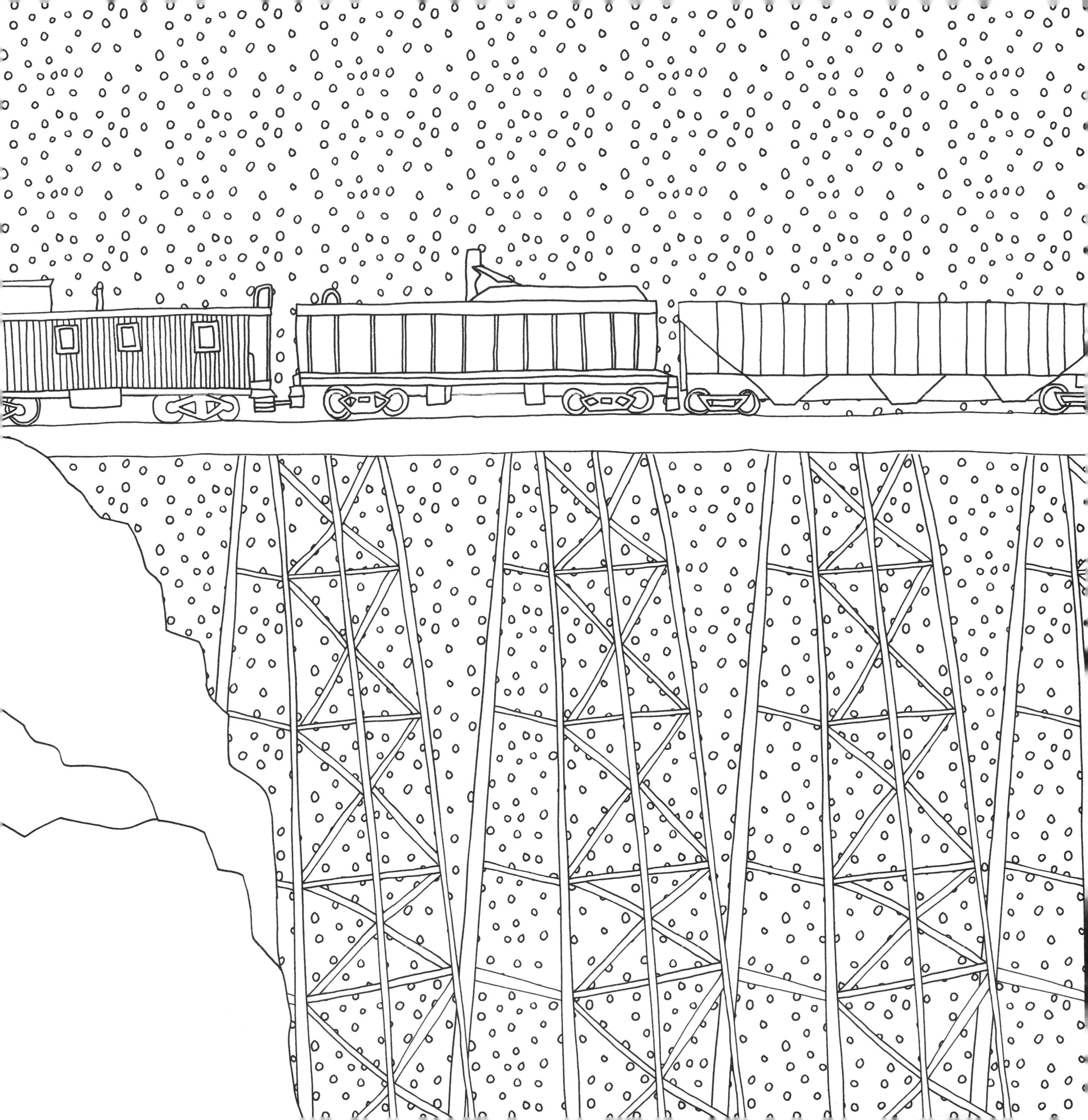

Cheese!

WISCONSIN

IOWA

MICHIGAN

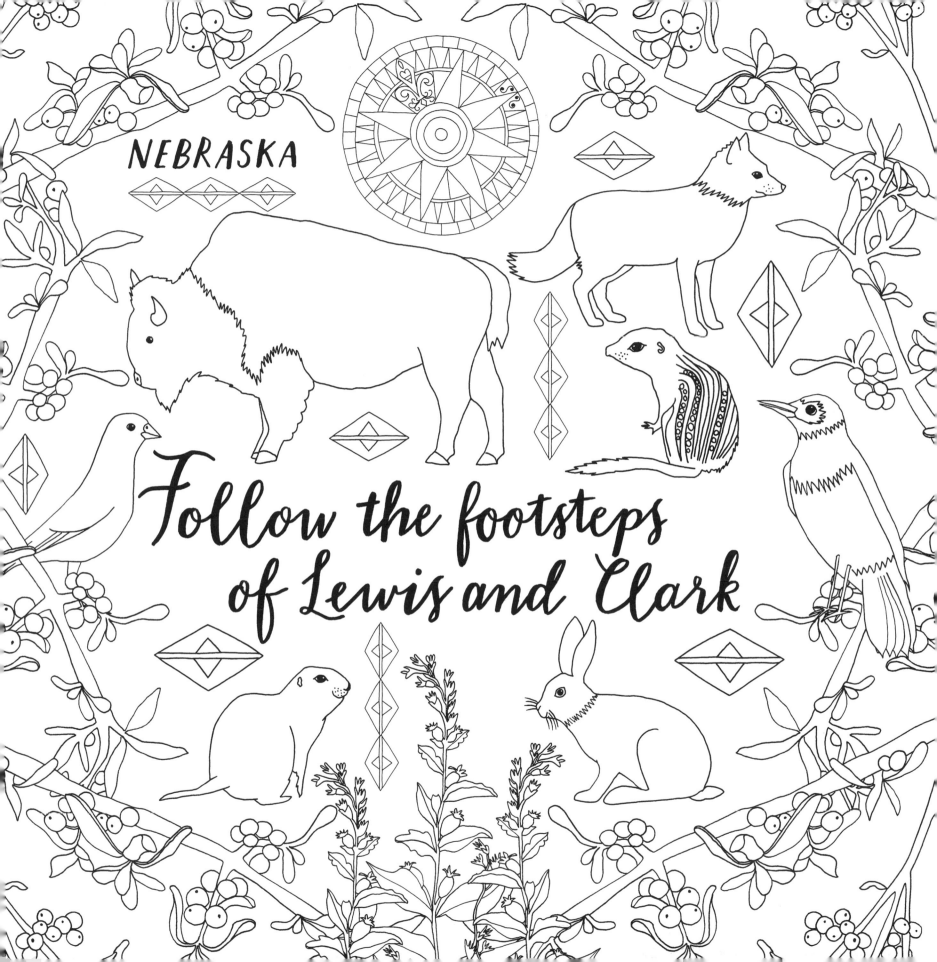

NEBRASKA

Follow the footsteps of Lewis and Clark

MEET ME IN ST. LOUIS

MISSOURI

ILLINOIS

HEAR the ROAR of the RACETRACK

INDIANA

I travel not to go anywhere,
but to go.
I travel for travel's sake.
— Robert Louis Stevenson

NEW HAMPSHIRE

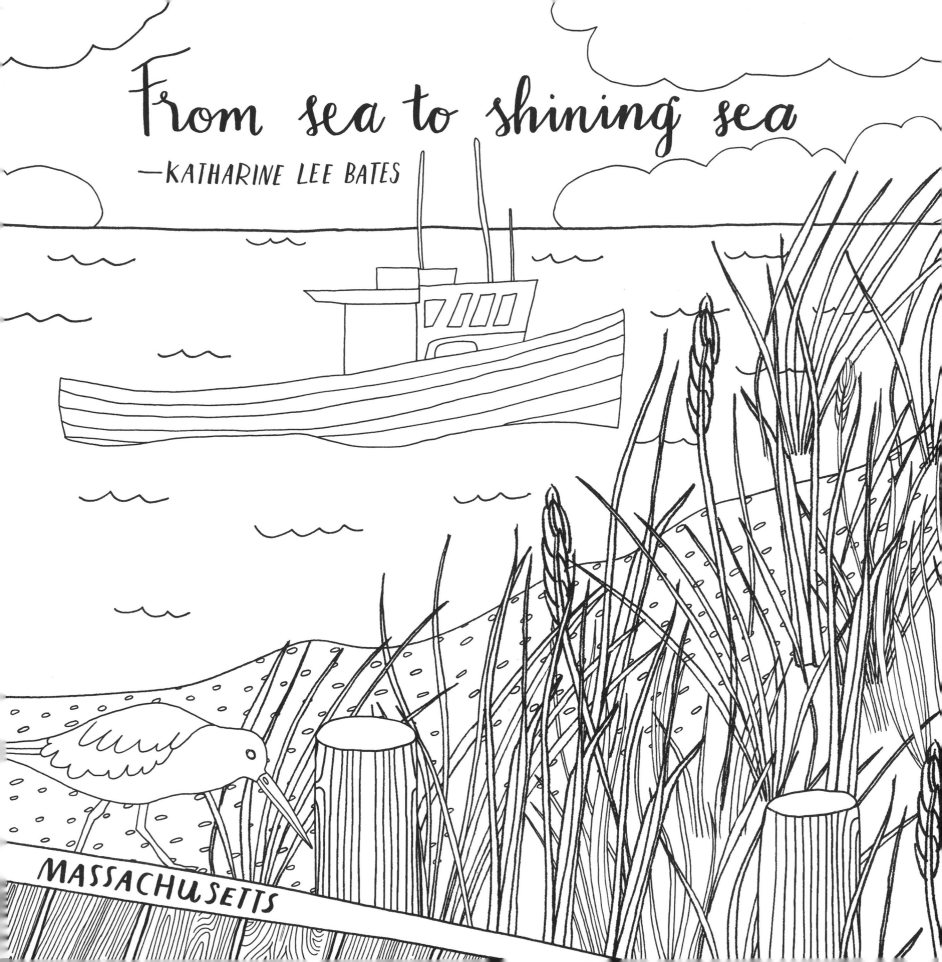

CONNECTICUT

NEW JERSEY

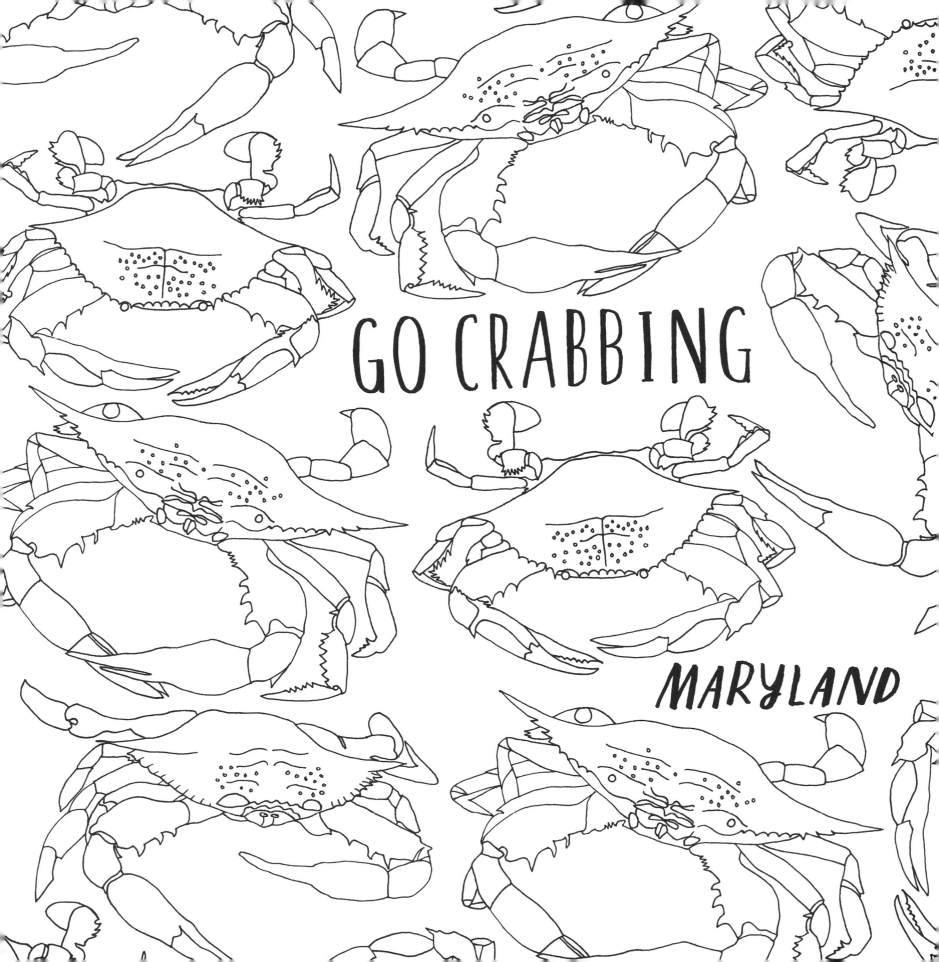

GO CRABBING

MARYLAND

Visit the pandas
at the national zoo

Take Me Home, Country Roads

—JOHN DENVER AND BILL & TAFFY DANOFF

WEST VIRGINIA

VIRGINIA

See the Chincoteague
wild ponies

SOUTHEAST

Hear pickin' at the Grand Ole Opry

TENNESSEE

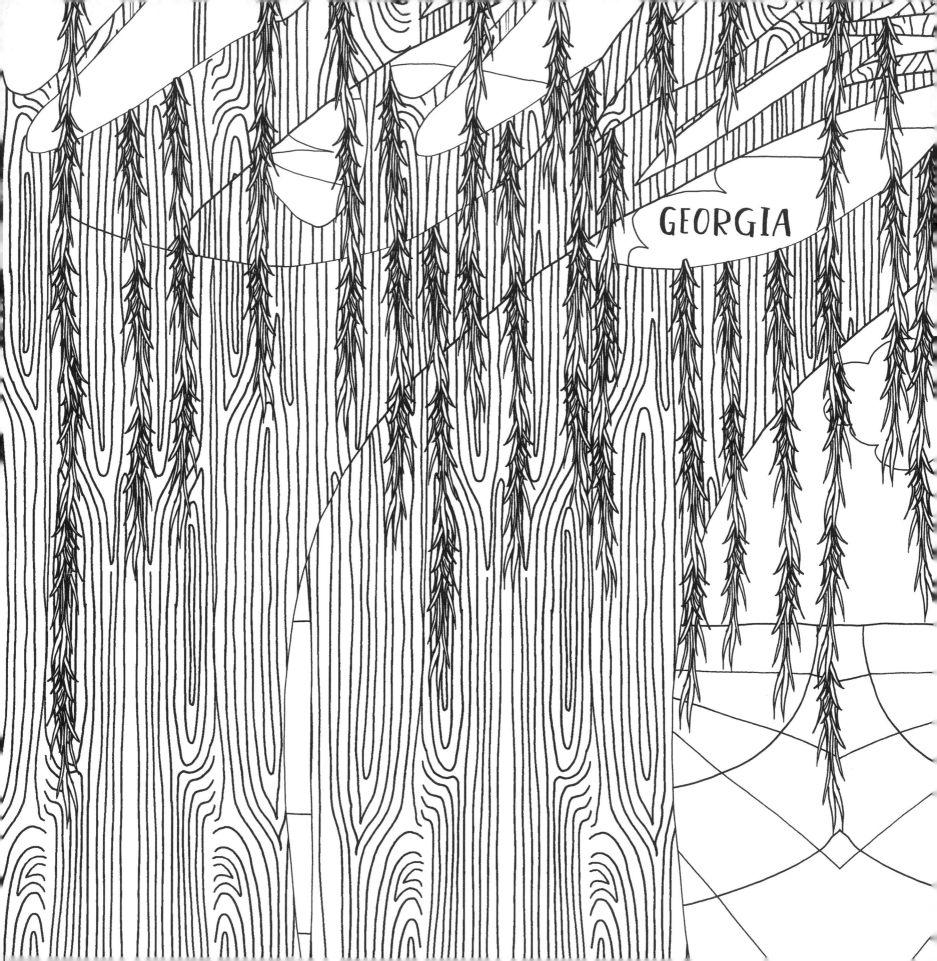

Take a step
into a hidden garden

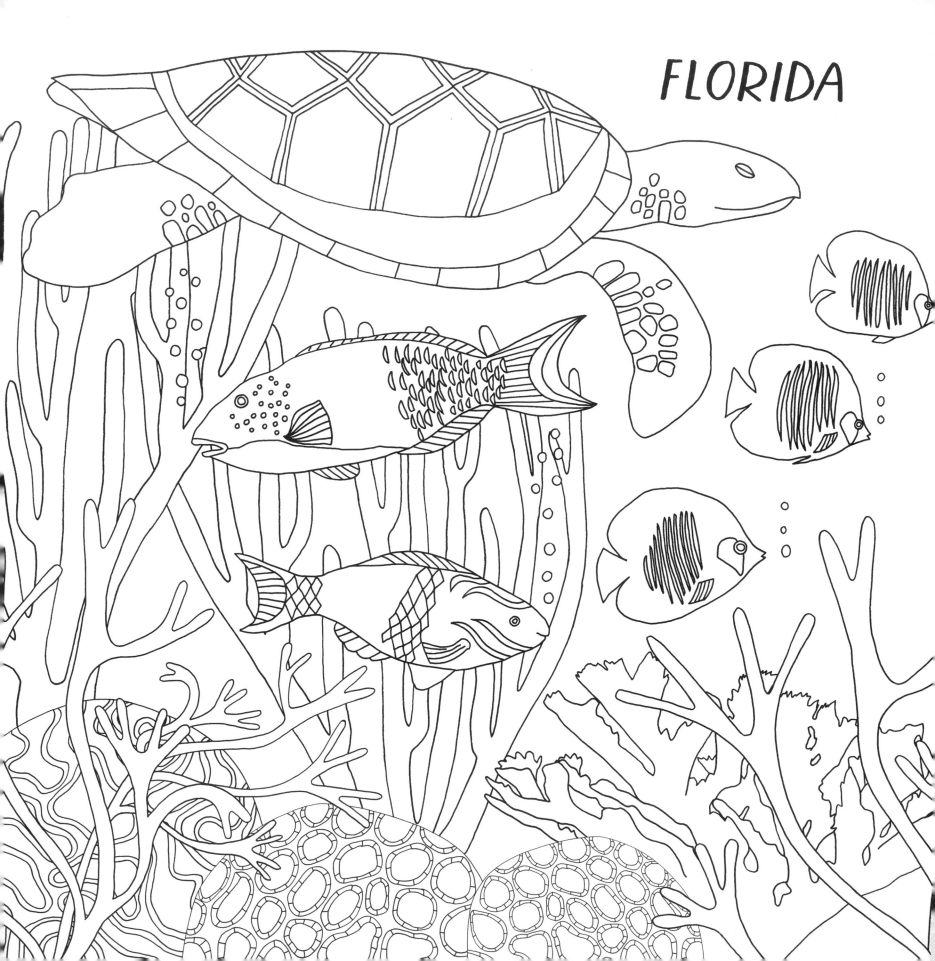

FLORIDA

About the Author

I have always loved art. My favorite thing in school was always the art projects—I spent as much time as I could in the art department. And, sure enough, I grew up to study textile design in college. My school focused on every part of the process, from the mechanical act of weaving fabric to the chemistry behind the dyes to the best part, the art of color and pattern.

Since my days at college, I've freelanced and worked at a bunch of other jobs. Now I work as a full-time illustrator—a job I love because I never know what's around the corner and no two days are the same!

List of Quotes

"O beautiful for spacious skies"—Katharine Lee Bates

"Free as the road"—George Herbert

"This Land Is Your Land"—Woody Guthrie

"I travel not to go anywhere, but to go. I travel for travel's sake."—Robert Louis Stevenson

"I hear America singing."—Walt Whitman

"Take Me Home, Country Roads"—John Denver and Bill & Taffy Danoff